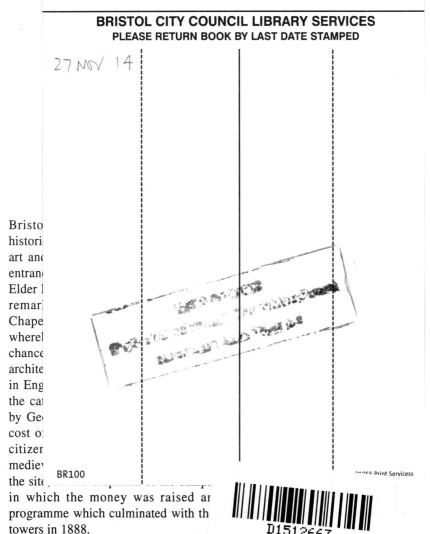

Bristo
histori
art and
entran
Elder I
remar
Chape
where
chance
archite
in Eng
the ca
by Ge
cost o
citizen
medie
the site

in which the money was raised ar
programme which culminated with th
towers in 1888.

The Augustinian Abbey

The Augustinian abbey was founded in 1140 by Robert Fitzharding, a
prominent Bristol citizen who later became Lord Berkeley; during the
next few decades the new foundation was well endowed with lands
and property in Bristol, Somerset and Gloucestershire.[2] It was the

1

income from these lands which enabled the Augustinian canons to carry out the successive building campaigns on their church, cloisters and the domestic buildings within the monastic precinct throughout the later Middle Ages. Gradually the original twelfth-century church was superseded by a larger and much more ambitious building. The chancel with its remarkable vaulted roof was begun during the time of Abbot Edmund Knowle (1307–1332) and the work was completed during the first half of the fourteenth century, including the Berkeley and Newton chapels attached to the south choir aisle. Work was interrupted by the Black Death of 1348–49 which affected Bristol very badly, killing between 35 and 40 per cent of the population. Further progress in replacing the original Norman work was made during the fifteenth century, and by the time of Abbot Newland or Nailheart (1481–1515) the north transept and the central tower had been completed and work started on rebuilding the nave. But the walls of this final phase in the reconstruction of the abbey church had only reached the lower part of the windows by 1539 when the abbey was suppressed, the Augustinian canons departed, and all further work ceased.[3] Abbot Newland kept a chronicle giving details of the history of the abbey, of earlier building work, and of his own contribution to the monastic architecture. This chronicle was continued after Newland's death in 1515, and records that work on the new nave had reached 'as high as the sills of the windows on the north side and at the west end'.[4]

Cathedral and Diocese of Bristol

In 1542 the diocese of Bristol was created as one of six new dioceses founded by Henry VIII. It consisted of Bristol and some nearby parishes, together with the county of Dorset which had previously been part of the diocese of Salisbury. The former Augustinian abbey church in Bristol became the cathedral of the new diocese, but by this time the original nave had been demolished and soon after the incomplete walls of the new nave were also destroyed, and for the next three centuries Bristol cathedral did not possess a nave. A wall was built to close off the western end of the transepts and the cathedral consisted only of the chancel and eastern Lady Chapel together with the side chapels, providing very inadequate accommodation for congregations. During the later sixteenth century several houses were erected on the site of the former nave, and by the mid-seventeenth century the area between the truncated cathedral and the former abbey gatehouse was crowded with houses including, on the south-west, a large building known as Minster House.[5] Many of these houses were occupied by the cathedral clergy and by officials such as the sexton, schoolmaster and organist, and they are listed in a detailed survey of the Chapter estates made by order of Parliament in 1649.[6] Throughout the seventeenth and eighteenth centuries visitors to Bristol commented unfavourably about the truncated state of the cathedral and its lack of a nave to match the architectural interest of its chancel. For example three military gentlemen from Norwich who left an account of their stay in Bristol in 1634 mentioned the unfinished state of the cathedral but remarked that the existing part 'may . . . compare for strength and beauty with any other'. They also commented upon the attractiveness of College Green 'with many shady trees, and most delightful walkes, about which stands many stately buildings (besides the Bishops Palace, the Deanes, the Chancellors, and the Prebends Houses) wherein many Gentlemen and Gentlewomen of note and ranke doe live'. Within the cathedral they were impressed by the recently-restored Organ and 'indifferent good Quiristers'.[7] Likewise Samuel Gale writing of a visit to Bristol with some friends in 1705 mentions that the cathedral 'wants half its length' although he was told quite erroneously that the nave had been demolished during the Civil War. He also remarked that there were 'no considerable monuments' within the cathedral, 'most of the bishops having been translated to other sees'.[8] Within the cathedral itself, congregations had to be accommodated in the cramped space provided by the transepts and the western end of the chancel. The altar was situated at the east end of the Lady Chapel, the choir stalls were moved eastward, and a stone screen or pulpitum which had formerly stood within the church of the White Friars in Bristol and had been given to the new cathedral in 1542 by Thomas White, a Bristol merchant, was erected east of the crossing.[9] This internal arrangement is shown on a plan of the cathedral made by Browne Willis in 1727. In his account of the cathedral, which was part of a survey of English cathedrals, Browne Willis commented on the small size and the unsatisfactory, cramped interior of Bristol Cathedral, although he did go on to praise the excellent way in which the building was maintained. He wrote that ' . . . the Example of this chapter is worthy to be recommended to the Imitation of our richest and most ancient Cathedrals'.[10] He also mentioned numerous buildings which were crowded on to the site of the former nave.

The Site of the Nave

By the early eighteenth century, however, there were some among the cathedral clergy who felt strongly about the impropriety of allowing houses and domestic offices to be built on the consecrated ground of the former nave. There had been protests against the renewal of leases on these houses during the 1630s, and in 1712 some of the canons again opposed the granting of leases on the grounds that

'. . . part of the Houses now contracted for is built upon Consecrated Ground and that which either has been or was designed to be part of the very body of the Church which is visible by some Pillars and ancient Monuments thereof now standing therein. And some part of the same has been and is at this time employed to the most sordid uses, such as Houses of Office and the like, besides some Chimnies built up against the Walls of the Church which not only annoy but impair and endanger the Fabrick'.[11]

In spite of these protests the leases were granted, although under various restrictions and conditions and the houses remained crowded on the site throughout the eighteenth century. By the early nineteenth century the canons and most of the cathedral staff preferred to live elsewhere, and many of the houses were let out to people who had no connection with the cathedral. In 1829 further leases were refused by the Dean and Chapter on the grounds that the houses had become 'very notoriously a Receptacle for Prostitutes'. The crowded houses on the site of the former nave, built over the north range of the cloisters, and packed into all the available space to the south and west up to the medieval gatehouse, are clearly shown in numerous early nineteenth-century drawings, notably in the Braikenridge collection at the City Museum and Art Gallery. By the 1830s many of these houses were obviously in very poor condition and those occupying the area of the former nave were finally demolished in 1838.[12]

As part of the major reorganisation of the Church of England during 1836–37, the diocese of Bristol was united with Gloucester, the Dorset part of the diocese returning to the diocese of Salisbury. Both Bristol and Gloucester retained their cathedrals and each had its own Dean and Chapter, but of Bristol it was unkindly said that it had 'half a Bishop and half a Cathedral.' The population of Bristol increased dramatically during the nineteenth century, more than doubling between 1801 and 1851, and rising to nearly 340,000 by 1901, so that the cramped and limited accommodation available for congregations in the cathedral became more and more unsatisfactory, and when in 1850 Gilbert Elliot became Dean of Bristol he resolved to do something to improve the situation.

Elliot was to remain at Bristol as Dean until his death in 1891 at the age of 91. He was a prominent low churchman who resolutely opposed any of the ecclesiastical ceremonial and ornaments favoured by the

Minster House and the central tower of the Cathedral from the south-west by Hugh O'Neill 1821 (from the Braikenbridge Collection, M1750, Bristol City Museum and Art Gallery).

Tractarian movement, and who refused to allow a cross, candles or flowers on the cathedral altars or a robed choir. A scholarly and respected figure, he was Prolocutor or 'speaker' of the Lower House of Convocation 1857–64, and in Bristol he played a prominent part in the founding of the University College and in raising funds for it during the 1870s, becoming the first President of the College, a position which he continued to hold until his death in 1891. He was also the first president of Clifton High School for Girls, founded in 1877.[13]

The Restoration of 1860

In order to provide more space for congregations in the cathedral, Elliot consulted the well-known architect and church restorer Giles Gilbert Scott. Scott took the view that 'the primary demand is for a nave of the grandest possible capacity' and recommended the removal of the Tudor Screen on which the organ stood, the clearance of many of the choir stalls and the provision of chairs for the congregation, thus increasing the available accommodation from some 300 persons to about 1000. Subscriptions were raised in Bristol and the work was carried out by the Bristol architect T.S. Pope in 1860–61 at a cost of more than £15,000. Unfortunately this major re-ordering of the interior resulted in the destruction of most of the beautiful screen or pulpitum which had been given to the cathedral in 1542, and the removal of the heraldic pavement from the Berkeley chapel. Elliot also seized the opportunity to remove and destroy some of the medieval misericords or lively carvings beneath the seats in the choir stalls which he regarded as indecent or improper, although from surviving illustrations they do not seem to have been particularly objectionable.[14] The result of Dean Elliot's work did not meet with universal approval. The Bishop of the diocese, Charles Thomas Baring, whose relations with the Dean and Chapter were already strained, opposed the scheme and refused to preach at the civic service held at the completion of the work on 27 June 1861, while the influential journal *The Ecclesiologist*, although acknowledging the difficulty of providing more space within the cathedral, totally condemned the way in which the scheme had been carried out, and suggested that it would have been far better to raise funds to rebuild the nave. In particular the journal criticised Pope's work in the strongest terms 'the pattern and materials are such as would disgrace a railway station, or the showroom of a cheap lath and plaster warehouse', while the verdict on the light screen which Pope had designed to replace the Tudor pulpitum was that it resembled 'a gate to a field with the hedges taken away'.[15]

The Reconstruction of the Nave

Soon after the re-opening of the cathedral in 1861, the condition of the central tower began to cause great concern. The removal of many of the buildings from the site of the former nave in 1838 meant that there was little support for the tower on the west side and an expensive scheme to provide massive buttresses was proposed. These necessary works were soon superseded by the more ambitious plan to rebuild the nave. There had already been several proposals for a new nave, and in particular a Bristol architect, Thomas Willson, had prepared an elaborate scheme during the 1830s with which he proposed to complete the nave according to the intentions of the late-medieval builders, although Willson's published designs, now in the City Art Gallery, show very elaborate ornamentation, with numerous pinnacles, elaborate tracery and carving, together with two curious octagonal towers at the west end. None of these proposals made much progress, however, and final success during the 1860s owed much to the energy, enthusiasm and fundraising efforts of John Pilkington Norris (1823–1891). He had been educated at Rugby under the great headmaster, Thomas Arnold, and at Trinity College, Cambridge; he became a Fellow of Trinity and was ordained priest in 1850. During the next few years he played a prominent part in the establishment of church schools and training colleges, and after holding various benefices he became a canon of Bristol cathedral in 1864. He was also vicar of St George's, Brandon Hill and later, in 1877 became vicar of St Mary Redcliffe. In 1881 he was appointed archdeacon of Bristol. During his years in Bristol he became greatly attached to the cathedral, writing on its history and raising very large sums for its enlargement.[16]

The idea of reconstructing the cathedral nave was given additional impetus in 1865–6 when work on a new road through College Green along the north side of the cathedral and through the site of the former Deanery revealed some of the foundations of Abbot Newland's proposed nave and north porch.[17] Dean Elliot had already left the Deanery on the curious grounds that it was unhealthy and had gone to live at 39 Royal York Crescent in Clifton. The Dean's wife had died in 1853 and in 1863 he married Frances Geils who had divorced her first husband, John Geils, a Scottish landowner. She was the daughter of Charles Dickinson of Queen Charlton, a member of the wealthy Quaker family with numerous connections in Bristol and the west country. She was an inveterate traveller, writing several accounts of her journeys; one of the daughters by her first marriage was married to the Marquis del Moral in Spain and another, Clothilde, became the Marchese Zondadari Chigi of Siena. After his second marriage Dean Elliot spent a good deal of time accompanying his wife on her travels and visits to her daughters and was away from Bristol for long periods.[18] In July 1866 Canon Norris wrote an address to the citizens of Bristol which was published in the local newspapers, appealing for subscriptions for the enormous task of building a new nave for the cathedral. As a result a committee was formed in October 1866 under the chairmanship of Henry Cruger William Miles of Kingsweston House, and with William Killigrew Wait of Clifton as its energetic secretary. W.K. Wait was a public-spirited merchant and philanthropist. He was Mayor during 1869–70 and represented Gloucester as an M.P. during 1873–74. The committee also included the Mayor, the High Sheriff, the Master of the Society of Merchant Venturers and such prominent Bristolians as Philip Miles, C.J. Monk M.P., W.F. Mogg, Francis Adams, J.B. Harford, W.H. Wills and several others. The speed with which the committee pressed ahead with its work is most impressive, and it is clear that the scheme appealed to the civic pride of many wealthy Bristolians and to their desire that the size of their cathedral should match the prestige and importance of the city. Within a few weeks subscriptions amounting to more than £11,000 were raised, and early in November 1866 Cruger Miles wrote to the Dean and Chapter requesting their support on the grounds that 'the imperfect state of your venerable cathedral is to some extent a subject of reproach to the City and its Citizens . . . ' The Dean doubted whether Bristolians would contribute the necessary funds, but had no objection to the scheme. A special meeting of the Chapter was called on 28 November 1866, and although the majority envisaged a very small nave of two or three bays only, they were content to leave the matter in the hands of the committee and resolved that 'the Chapter is willing to leave all the arrangements as to choice of the Architect to the Committee'. They did, however, insist 'on the new fabric being in the same style of Architecture as the old'.[19] Thereafter, apart from Canon Norris, the Chapter took very little part in the project for several years, Dean Elliot and most of the Chapter remained aloof from it, and surviving correspondence shows that relations between the Dean and Canon Norris remained icily correct but were never cordial.

The Committee pressed ahead with great speed, and in December 1866 appointed as its architect George Edmund Street (1824–81) who was already known for his Gothic designs for churches, schools and

George Edmund Street's proposal for the west front (from *The Architect,*
23 September 1876).

public buildings. In 1864 he had designed All Saints', Clifton, which, like many of his churches, was well suited to a Tractarian style of worship, a fact which can hardly have recommended him to Dean Elliot.[20] Within a month Street had examined the site and prepared a preliminary report. Since he had found ample evidence of the late-medieval foundations and it was clear from these what size the nave would have reached if it had been completed, Street felt it proper to adhere to this original plan as closely as possible, and also to follow, though not slavishly to copy, the architectural style of the fourteenth-century choir. Dundry stone had been used for the original building, but since large quantities were no longer available Street decided to use Doulting stone for the new nave with Lias supports for the pillars instead of the Purbeck stone used by the medieval builders.[21] His son later wrote that

'. . . my father felt that there was really no course open to him but to build on the old foundations and on the same lines as the choir, and to make the distinction between the old and new work in the details, such as a greater elaboration of the mouldings, a variety in the window-traceries and in the character of the sculpture, and a different treatment of the groining. He also made fresh designs for all the monumental recesses which, following the old model, he introduced under the aisle windows.'[22]

Street's design also included two western towers, since although these were not part of the medieval plan, he felt that they would add dignity to the building and emphasise its importance as a cathedral.

Meanwhile the committee continued to be extremely active and successful in raising money for the project which had obviously captured the enthusiasm of many Bristolians.

Among the multitude of contributors, large sums were donated from Canon Norris and from other members of the committee. Other generous donors included J.H. Greville Smyth, of Ashton Court, Thomas Daniel of Berkeley Square, several members of the Miles family of Kingsweston and Abbots Leigh, the Society of Merchant Venturers, Stuckey's Bank, Robert Bright and William Gibbs, as well as innumerable smaller contributions from less wealthy Bristol citizens.[23] The speed with which the necessary large sums of money were raised and the evident enthusiasm for the project was extremely impressive. Partly this was due to civic pride and a desire that Bristol should have a cathedral in keeping with its status as an historic city and a prosperous port. One contributor wrote the he wished 'to remove a stigma of long standing from the citizens of Bristol'. Inevitably not everyone was in favour however, and some who were approached for

10

contributions refused, giving reasons such as 'I cannot persuade myself to feel any interest . . . not seeing to what use it can be put except it be for processions', or opposing 'the restoration of these monuments of other times, so well fitted for Roman Catholic worship and so little adapted to Protestant worship . . .'

Notwithstanding such views, money poured in, and on 1 October 1867 a contract for executing the first part of the work according to Street's designs was agreed with George William Booth, builder, of Gosport, Hampshire, who had made a tender of £14,270. Preliminary work on the site proceeded rapidly under the supervision of George Wall, the clerk of works, and by 17 April 1868 the foundation stone of the new nave could be laid. An elaborate ceremony took place in the presence of Charles John Ellicott, Bishop of Gloucester and Bristol, accompanied by a large number of clergy, as well as by civic dignitaries, members of the Committee and by no less than 300 Free Masons headed by the Earl of Limerick, the Provincial Grand Master, who laid the foundation stone on the site of the north-west tower with much symbolic ritual and solemnity. By 1871 £23,000 had been raised, of which £20,000 had already been spent, and by 1874 the subscriptions totalled £39,500 and expenditure had reached £32,500, while 22 men were regularly employed with many more casual labourers.[24]

Work continued steadily during the next few years and the Committee remained active and successful in raising a continuous supply of money for the project, so that by 1876 the new nave was virtually complete and was ready to be used for public worship, although the two western towers had not been finished. Meanwhile on 12 October 1875 another public meeting was held and another committee was formed whose purpose was to raise a further sum of money to build the north-west tower of the cathedral to Street's designs as a memorial to Bishop Joseph Butler, the noted theologian, who had been bishop of Bristol from 1738 to 1750. The sum required was £3,000, and again Canon Norris agreed to be Treasurer. Within eighteen months the Committee for the North-West Tower had received contributions totalling £1,675 11s 0d towards the cost of the project and work had commenced. Later, the South-West Tower was to be completed and dedicated to the memory of the Bristol philanthropist, Edward Colston (1636–1721).[25]

Controversy and Discord

Up to this time relations between the Committee, the architect and the Cathedral Chapter had remained amicable, largely thanks to the fact

11

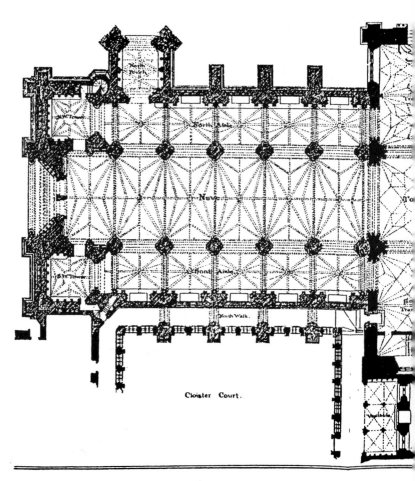

George Edmund Street's plan of the Cathedral, showing the medieval cha
(from *The Arc*

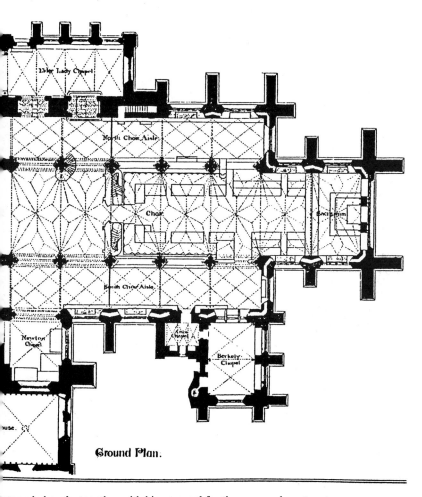

Elder Lady Chapel

North Choir Aisle

Choir

Sacristium

South Choir Aisle

Newton Chapel

Berkely Chapel

house.

Ground Plan.

...pts and chapels, together with his proposal for the nave and western towers
...ptember 1876).

that, apart from Canon Norris, the Dean and Chapter appeared to take very little close interest in the work. Early in 1876, however, this happy state of affairs was rudely shattered. William Killigrew Wait who had been such a hard-working and successful secretary to the Committee had decided to crown his major contributions to the work on the nave by giving some £1,200 for the building of the north porch. This was designed by Street who provided niches for statues around the entrance. The task of making the statues and the choice of subjects was left to the sculptor, James Frank Redfern (1838–76), who had worked closely with Street for many years. Redfern was responsible for carving many of the statues on the west front of Salisbury cathedral, and he had also provided statues for several of the churches which Street had built in the East Riding of Yorkshire for the benevolent landowner, Sir Tatton Sykes. In Bristol Redfern had carved the elaborate reredos for Street's church of All Saints', Clifton in 1864. Redfern's statues were placed in their niches around the porch in February 1876. They included the Virgin Mary alone and the Virgin Mary and the Christ Child at the apex, and the figures of the four Latin Doctors – St Gregory, St Ambrose, St Jerome and St Augustine. Each of the large figures was distinguished by their traditional attributes, so that St Gregory was crowned with a papal tiara, St Ambrose carried a triple scourge, St Jerome had his cardinal's hat and St Augustine carried a burning heart. Since the figures were arranged around the doorway, all the details were clearly visible, and their appearance led to a stream of protest from those who feared the creeping influence of Catholicism in the Church of England, and all the latent forces of anti-popery and protestantism were roused to violent anger. Dean Elliot was on an extended holiday in Italy and Street was also abroad, but the local papers were filled with letters of protest and virulent anti-Catholic feeling, and, at a well-attended meeting held in the Colston Hall on 3 April 1876 'to protest against the imagery lately erected outside Bristol cathedral' very strong passions were displayed and violent speeches were made condemning the statues. A resolution was passed by a large majority demanding that they be removed immediately. So great was the excitement engendered by the fear of popery within the Church that some even claimed to detect in the statue of St Jerome the features of the renegade Anglican John Henry Newman.[26]

When Dean Elliot returned to Bristol a meeting of the Chapter was held on 4 April 1876 at which petitions and protests against the statues were presented on behalf of the public meeting and from the low-church Clerical and Lay Evangelical Association, which existed to preserve the Protestant tradition and character of the Church of England and to resist all attempts to introduce Catholic practices. In spite of the strong objections by Canon John Norris and Canon Nugent Wade, the Chapter resolved that

'the Dean be requested to take such measures as he may think fit for removing the objectionable Statues from the north porch of the new nave of the Cathedral'.[27]

Without consulting either the Committee or the architect, and without waiting for a judicial ruling from an ecclesiastical court on the legality of the statues, the Dean engaged a gang of workmen who, early one morning, tore the offending statues from their niches. One Bristol newspaper reported that 'a more rough and open exhibition of iconoclasm has not been seen in Bristol since the days of Oliver Cromwell'.[28] In the process of removal the Virgin Mary was badly damaged, but the other statues could be repaired and still survive since they were rescued by Street and used to adorn the tower of the church at East Heslerton in the East Riding of Yorkshire on which he was engaged at the time. In 1878 the empty niches in the cathedral porch were filled with the figures of the four Evangelists.

The Dean's precipitate action provoked a vigorous protest from G.E. Street who wrote to the Dean and to *The Guardian* newspaper, complaining that the Dean had hitherto taken no interest in the work or any of the details, and discussing at some length the whole question of sculptures on churches and how far it was reasonable to represent the saints by their usual symbols and by conventional but unhistorical dress. To the Dean he wrote that drawings of the proposed porch and its statues had been widely distributed since 1867,

'But you will excuse my saying that, seeing with what singular care you avoided discussing anything connected with the new works with me, I should have thought it a grave impertinence to ask your opinion of any of the details. I gathered from your manner you did not much like the work being undertaken, nor cared to make yourself in any way responsible for the character of any portion of it. You left all the responsibility, both for the cost and execution of my designs, to the Committee . . . '.[29]

Street went on to point out that 'The designs of the figures were not mine, but those of the sculptor, Mr Redfern, who executed them'. Street stated that he was abroad when the figures were put up, and that he felt that 'Mr Redfern, the sculptor, was injudicious in making so much of some of the insignia of the four doctors'. But the details, and in particular the cardinal's hat and the papal tiara could easily have been altered, 'and these alterations could be made even now if the statues have not been damaged (as I am informed they have been) by the careless and hasty way in which your removal of them was effected'.[30]

The unfortunate sculptor, James Redfern, who found himself held responsible by all sides in this passionate controversy, was devastated by the uproar his artistic work had created. Although only thirty-eight years of age, he retreated from all further involvement, fell ill and died later in the same year. Meanwhile the committee, who had worked so successfully to raise the money and organise the work of re-building the nave, felt gravely insulted by the action of the Dean and Chapter and by the peremptory removal of the figures without any reference to them, more especially since the money for the porch had been the generous gift of their hard-working secretary, W.K. Wait. On 18 April 1876, therefore, all the members of the committee resigned, and wrote to the Chapter stating 'That as the Dean expresses no regret for the outrage which has been committed or for the discourtesy offered as well to the donor of the porch as to the eminent architect who has been engaged in the work, but rather justifies the steps that have been taken . . . ', they would take no further part in the completion of the nave. They also pointed out that whereas the Dean had been indifferent to their efforts to rebuild the nave, he had acted with great vigour and undue haste in defacing 'a very beautiful work of art'.[31] Canon Norris was deeply upset by the controversy and by the offence caused to the Committee of which he had been the Treasurer. In his surviving notes he records that he considered resigning his position as a Canon because of his 'strong feelings of indignation' at the way he considered the Committee had been treated. In the event he retained his office, although only after an angry exchange of letters with the Dean. Thereafter the relations between the two men, which had never been cordial, were even more distant, and their antagonism spilt over into disagreements about the frequency of services in the Cathedral, the conduct of Holy Communion, the observance of the rubrics in the Book of Common Prayer and other occasions of dispute.[32]

The Dean and Chapter were left with no alternative but to supervise the completion of the work themselves. A 'Cathedral Completion Fund' with the Dean as Treasurer was opened and further donations were sought to provide the further sum of £3,608 which was needed, but after all the controversy and without the energy, enthusiasm and influence of the committee, money came in slowly. Those who had been in the forefront when raising the cry of 'No Popery' were much less prominent when contributions were requested, and it was only after considerable delay that enough money was raised so that the

View from the south-east during the construction of the new nave. Photographed about 1878, this shows the almost-completed nave but without the western towers and with the central tower unrestored. Note the mason's yard with the open-fronted lodge and piles of scaffolding (from Dr Warwick Rodwell).

nave, still without its western towers, could be opened for public worship. This period also saw further difficulties between the Dean and Canon Norris. The popularity and influence of Canon Norris meant that he was much more successful in raising money than the Dean or the other members of the Chapter, and he was urged by the Dean not to continue his fund-raising in Bristol for the North-West tower so as not to compete with the Cathedral Completion Fund. The Dean wrote that 'a special canvass now would but revive jealousies, rivalries, misrepresentations and antagonisms which have already done much mischief and ought to be discouraged, not encouraged'.

Completion of the Work

In spite of these problems, however, sufficient money was raised for the completion of the nave, and on 23 October 1877 the opening service was held in the presence of the Bishop of Gloucester and Bristol, the Bishop of Bath and Wells, the Dean of Canterbury and Westminster and a great gathering of clergy and civic dignitaries. Sadly, however, only a few of the committee who had worked so successfully for this outcome were present. Their efforts had raised some £48,000 up to that time.[33]

With the nave in use, work on the exterior and the two western towers continued more slowly. George Edmund Street, who had designed the new nave to blend so harmoniously with the remarkable medieval choir, died on 18 December 1881. He was succeeded as architect to the project by John Loughborough Pearson (1817–97) who was already well-known for the design and restoration of cathedrals and churches all over the country, and who had been appointed architect of the new cathedral at Truro.[34] At Bristol Pearson was responsible for finishing the western towers and the west front of the cathedral; he re-arranged the choir with a new marble floor, designed the reredos for the high altar, the sedelia and the crossing screen; he also restored the ancient gateway to the abbey precinct with its fine Romanesque archways. In completing Street's work on the exterior Pearson adhered to the original plan, only omitting the two steeples which Street had envisaged as capping the western towers.

By 1882 the progress of the work on the west end meant that the remaining buildings to the west had to be removed. There were three main buildings in the area. One was the Chapter Office, the second was the large house at the south-west corner known as Minster House and the third was the medieval gate house with the precentor's house adjoining. Minster House stood on the site of and incorporated some

18

parts of the medieval prior's lodging; its foundations were revealed during the archaeological excavation in 1992. In April 1882 the Chapter received a report from J.L. Pearson suggesting that the Chapter Office and Minster House should be demolished, that the precentor's house should be removed and that the medieval gatehouse should be restored 'to the condition of its best period'.[35]

Finally in 1882 after twenty years of work and intensive fund-raising the whole project was completed and on 8 June 1888 the opening ceremony took place before a congregation of some 3,000 people and with the cathedral lit by electric light.[36] Two weeks later a Service of Thanksgiving was held to celebrate the completion of the work and the sermon was preached by the Bishop of Gloucester, Charles John Ellicott. In the notes which he helpfully provided for the bishop, the Dean, Gilbert Elliot, gave a brief account of the progress of the work from his installation in 1850 together with figures for money raised over the years. The Dean's figures do not agree in detail with those which are cited by some other authorities, but nonetheless they give some idea of the cost of the work and the extent of the fund-raising involved. The Dean's summary was as follows:

Date	Works	Money supplied by the Chapter	Money raised by Public Subscription	Total
1860	Restoration of Chancel and extension of accommodation	£7,393	£5,474	£12,867
1862	Further restoration	£6,315		£6,315
1866–76	Re-building the nave		£45,000	£45,000
1876–84	Further work on the nave		£6,465	£6,465
1882	Demolition of the Chapter Office and Minster House	£800		£800
1884–	Completion of the towers		£6,000	£6,000
	TOTAL Expenditure	£14,508	£62,939	£77,447

19

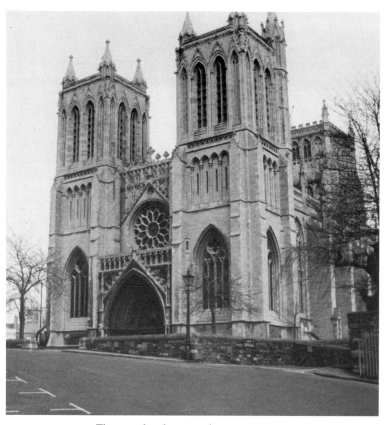

The completed nave and western towers.

The two men who, in spite of their frequently strained relations, had been closely involved in the reconstruction of the cathedral nave, Dean Gilbert Elliot and Canon John Pilkington Norris, both died in 1891. Gilbert Elliot was 91 years of age and had been Dean since 1850. For many years he had been a forceful and enterprising worker on behalf of the cathedral and of numerous other deserving causes in Bristol, although since he remained in office so long his last years were marked by controversies and he was said to have seldom been seen in the cathedral. Canon Norris was also a notable scholar, the author of numerous theological works and a great advocate of Church schools and training colleges. He had been Archdeacon of Bristol since 1881 and had been even more zealous as a supporter of good causes and as a fund raiser. He had thrown himself wholeheartedly into the project for the re-building of the cathedral nave and had proved to have a superb talent for obtaining subscriptions from wealthy persons in Bristol and beyond. He was also an active supporter of the campaign to restore the Bristol Diocese, and £5,000 was subscribed as a memorial to him to be devoted to the augmentation of the Bristol bishopric. Without his initiation of the project, continued support for it and energetic work in obtaining subscriptions it is unlikely that the cathedral nave would have been built.

Gilbert Elliot's successor as Dean was Francis Pigou who had previously been Dean of Chichester. He differed greatly from his predecessor, both in character and churchmanship, and one of his first actions was to place a cross, candlesticks and flowers on the cathedral altars and to provide the choir with cassocks and surplices. Canon Norris was chosen to replace him at Chichester and had accepted the appointment, but he died on 29 December 1891 before he could move from Bristol.

Many of those who had worked so hard for the enlargement of the cathedral dreamt of the restoration of the Bristol diocese as a suitable recognition of the wealth, importance and population of the city. The campaign for a Bristol bishopric had begun in 1877 with a public meeting and petition to the government. It received considerable impetus in 1883 when it gained the support of the Prime Minister, W.E. Gladstone, and subscriptions were invited to provide an endowment for the bishopric. Again, Canon Norris was involved in the fund-raising, and by July 1884 £20,000 had been obtained, and an Act of Parliament for a new diocese was passed. But the rights of the bishop of the united dioceses of Gloucester and Bristol had to be safeguarded, and it was not until 1897 that the object was finally achieved, by which time £70,000 had been subscribed. The composition of the new diocese owed little to logic or any natural cohesion and much to the route of the Great Western Railway, for as well as Bristol, it consisted of the parts of south Gloucestershire and north Wiltshire which could easily be reached by train. The first bishop of the new diocese, George Forrest Browne, was enthroned in Bristol cathedral, which was filled for the occasion by a very large congregation, on 28 October 1897.[38] With the nave completed, the interior of the cathedral reorganised and with the bishopric and diocese restored, the dreams of those who had laboured for so long and contributed so generously were finally realised.

Acknowledgements

I am grateful to Eric Boore, Francis Greenacre, Peter Harris, David Large, Nicholas Lee, Elizabeth Ralph, Michael Richardson, Dr Warwick Rodwell, Professor Robert Savage and Dr Michael Smith for their help and for providing information and illustrations.

References

1. Nikolaus Pevsner, *The Buildings of England: North Somerset and Bristol*, 1958, 372; Andor Gomme et al., *Bristol: An Architectural History*, 1979, 31–8; M.Q. Smith, *The Art & Architecture of St Augustine's Abbey now Bristol Cathedral*, 1991, 4–7.
2. J.C. Dickinson, 'The Origins of St Augustine's, Bristol', in P. McGrath & J. Cannon, eds., *Essays in Bristol & Gloucestershire History*, 1976, 109–126; G. Beachcroft and A. Sabin, eds., 'Two Compotus Rolls of St Augustine's Abbey, Bristol', *Bristol Record Society*, IX, 1938; A. Sabin, 'The Foundation of the Abbey of St Augustine at Bristol', *Bristol & Gloucestershire Archaeological Society Transactions*, 75, 1956, 35–42.
3. J.H. Bettey, *The Suppression of the Religious Houses in Bristol*, Bristol Branch, Historical Association, 1990.
4. I.H. Jeayes, ed., 'Abbot Newland's Roll', *Bristol & Gloucestershire Archaeological Society Transactions*, XIV, 1889–90, 130; R.W. Paul, 'The Plan of the Church and Monastery of St Augustine, Bristol', *Archaeologia*, 63, 191–2, 231–50.
5. The first lease was granted in 1583. Bristol Record Office, DC/A/7/9/1.
6. B.R.O. DC/E/3/2, Parliamentary Survey of the Capitular Estates, 1649; E. Boore, 'The Minster House – Bristol Cathedral', *Bristol and Avon Archaeology*, 9, 1990–91, 43–8.
7. L.G. Wickham Legg, ed., *A Relation of a Short Survey of 26 Counties, 1634*, 1904, 92–5.
8. Bristol University Library, Special Collection, Samuel Gale's MSS 'A Tour through Several Parts of England', 1705, 31–2. I am grateful to Michael Richardson for drawing this to my attention.
9. A. Sabin, 'The Tudor Screen' in Elizabeth Ralph & John Rogan, eds., *Essays in Cathedral History*, 1991, 41–2.
10. Browne Willis, *Survey of the English Cathedrals*, 1927, 758–62. A useful summary of the changes made to the cathedral during the seventeenth and eighteenth centuries, with informative illustrations and references, is G. Cobb, *English Cathedrals: The Forgotten Centuries*, 1980, 36–51.
11. B.R.O. DC/A/7/9/1.
12. B.R.O. DC/A/8/3–5; DC/A/&/9/1; Bristol City Museum & Art Gallery, Braikenridge Collection M1750–M1766; SOL 167.
13. J.A. Venn, *Alumni Cantabrigiensis 1752–1900*, 1944.
14. G.G. Scott, 'Report on Bristol Cathedral', 1859, British Library Add. MSS 31382; John Latimer, *Annals of Bristol in the Nineteenth Century*, 1887, Reprint 1990, 369–70.
15. *The Ecclesiologist*, XX, 1859, 330–32.
16. *Dictionary of National Biography*; J.P. Norris, 'Architectural History of Bristol Cathedral', *Bristol & Gloucestershire Archaeological Society Transactions*, 15, 1890–91, 61–80.

17. B.R.O. DC/A/8/7 Chapter Minutes 1858–79. See 19 September 1865.
18. They were married by licence at Queen Charlton. The marriage register describes the bride as 'Frances Dickinson, single', while the *Bristol Times* in reporting the marriage describes her as 'Mrs Dickinson, the lady of the manor of Queen Charlton'. A year earlier Dean Elliot had officiated at the marriage of one of her daughters at Queen Charlton. Somerset Record Office, D/P/Q Cha 2/1/4. *Bristol Times* 7 November 1863. Joy Burden, *Winging Westward*, 1974, 16.
19. *Bristol Gazette* 1 November 1866.
20. E. Ralph & P. Cobb, *New Anglican Churches in Nineteenth-Century Bristol*, Bristol Branch, Historical Association 1991; A.E. Street, *Memoir of George Edmund Street*, 1888.
21. I am grateful to Professor Robert Savage for inspecting the stone in the cathedral nave and for supplying me with information about it.
22. A.E. Street, *op. cit.*, 177.
23. B.R.O. DC/F/4/2/1 Ledger of Committee for Restoration of the Nave 1866–70; DC/F/1/3 Miscellaneous items relating to the Cathedral building and restoration 1860–1924.
24. B.R.O. DC/F/4/1 Fabric Fund Account Book 1866–75; DC/F/1/3 Miscellaneous letters and papers relating to the Cathedral 1860–1924; *Bristol Times* 17 April 1868; *Bristol Mercury* 18 April 1868.
25. B.R.O. DC/A/8/7 Chapter Minutes 1858–79; DC/A/8/16 Canon Norris's Notes 1865–91.
26. *Bristol Times* 4 April 1876.
27. B.R.O. DC/A/8/7; DC/A/8/16 Canon Norris's Notes 1865–91.
28. *Bristol Times* 7 April 1876.
29. A.E. Street, *op. cit.*, 180–1.
30. *Ibid.*
31. B.R.O. DC/A/8/7 Chapter Minutes 1858–79.
32. B.R.O. DC/A/8/16 Memoranda on Chapter Meetings compiled by Canon Norris 1865–1891.
33. B.R.O. DC/F/3/1a–b 10 January 1877; DC/F/1/3 22 January 1877; *Bristol Times* 24 October 1877.
34. A. Quinney, *John Loughborough Pearson*, 1979.
35. B.R.O. DC/A/8/8 Chapter Minutes 1879–1900; J. Latimer, *Annals of Bristol: Nineteenth Century*, 1887, reprinted 1970, 516; A. Quinney, *op. cit.*, 243–4. For details of the archaeological excavation see Eric Boore, 'Bristol Cathedral – Excavations in 1991–2', *Rescue News*, 1992, 6–7. See also Eric Boore 'Minster House', *Bristol & Avon Archaeology*, 9, 1990–1, 43–8.
36. *Bristol Times* 9 June 1888; J. Latimer, *op. cit.*, Part II, 8.
37. B.R.O. DC/F/1/4.
38. J. Latimer, *op. cit.*, Part I, 492; Part II, 39, 59.

George Edmund's Sketch of the view across the new nave (from the *Building News*, 2 September 1881).